The Way to God

The Way to God

Selected Writings from
Mahatma Gandhi

Edited by M. S. Deshpande
Foreword by Arun Gandhi
Introduction by Michael N. Nagler

[The original title of this work is *Pathway to God*.]

North Atlantic Books
Berkeley, California

Published by
North Atlantic Books
P.O. Box 12327
Berkeley, California 94712

Cover photo © Vithalbhai Jhaveri/GhandhiServe
Cover design by Paula Morrison
Printed in the United States of America

The Way to God is sponsored by the Society for the Study of Native Arts and Sciences, a nonprofit educational corporation whose goals are to develop an educational and cross-cultural perspective linking various scientific, social, and artistic fields; to nurture a holistic view of arts, sciences, humanities, and healing; and to publish and distribute literature on the relationship of mind, body, and nature.

North Atlantic Books' publications are available through most bookstores. For further information, visit our website at www.northatlanticbooks.com or call 800-733-3000.

Library of Congress Cataloging-in-Publication Data
Gandhi, Mahatma, 1869–1948
[Pathway to God]
The way to God / Mohandas K. Gandhi ; edited by M. S. Deshpande ; foreword by Arun Gandhi ; introduction by Michael N. Nagler.
    p. c.m.
Originally published: Berkeley, Calif. : Berkeley Hills Books, 1999.
Includes bibliographical references.
ISBN 978-1-55643-784-7
    1. Religious life—Hinduism. 2. Hinduism—Doctrines. I. Deshpande, M. S. (Manohar Srinivas), b 1899. II. Title.
BL1214.24.G36 2009
294.5'44—dc22
                                        2008043941

1 2 3 4 5 6 7 8 9 UNITED 14 13 12 11 10 09

Contents

Publisher's Note

The Way to God was edited by M. S. Deshpande and first published in India in 1971 under the title, *Pathway to God*. The main text was minimally altered for the present edition, with only a few revisions made in punctuation and spelling. Part titles have been changed, the prefatory essays have been replaced with new pieces that address American readers, and the Appendix has been omitted.

We would like to express our thanks to Vandana Shiva and the late Eknath Easwaran, who, through their ideas and writings, inspired this effort to bring the thought of Mahatma Gandhi to Western readers.

Foreword

ARUN GANDHI

When Grandfather confessed to his Christian friends how much he was impressed by the Sermon on the Mount he was asked, "Why don't you become a Christian?" "When you convince me that all Christians live according to the Sermon on the Mount, I will be the first to change my religion," he responded.

On another occasion he said religion is like a mother. However good your friend's mother may be, you cannot forsake your own. In the spirit of loving one's mother he chose to remain a Hindu; and also because of the liberty the philosophy afforded an individual. I call Hinduism a philosophy since it is neither an organized religion nor a way of life. It is based on faith and allows an individual the freedom to define one's own way of worship.

Hinduism is reputed to have more than fifty thousand deities, which does not necessarily mean Hindus believe there are as many Gods. It only means there are so many images of God, and since no one knows what the true image of God is, who can decry the image that someone holds close to the heart?

Gandhi preferred to work within Hinduism because only Hinduism would allow the form of universal worship that he practiced, incorporating, as he did, prayers and hymns from all major religions of the world. Most other organized religions would consider this a blasphemy. Yet, no one can deny that there is a vast difference between the essence, or the core, of the Hinduism that Gandhi discovered and adopted and what is practiced as a religion today.

He sincerely believed in the oneness of God—the images are different, the names are different, but God is one. I hope the essence of this message will come through his writings to the reader, and will be adequately understood and accepted by all of humanity so that we can understand and respect the different images of God.

Introduction

MICHAEL N. NAGLER

One day a British cleric well-known for his imperialistic persuasion found himself face to face with Mahatma Gandhi. Wishing to paper over their differences, he is said to have remarked, "Well, we're both men of God, Mr. Gandhi, aren't we?" "You are a politician disguised as a man of God," the Mahatma replied. "I am a man of God disguised as a politician." If this story is true—and it's true to character, at least—then this book is designed to help us see past the Mahatma's disguise.

We cannot emphasize too much, I think, that whereas his contribution as a political liberator was unique in world history, in the long run it may be his contribution to humanity's inner life that proves more important. The world needs a thorough political overhaul, but it is becoming clearer day by day that unless that overhaul is based on some kind of spiritual reawakening, it will only deposit us back in the same old dilemmas, sooner or later.

This selection from Gandhi's writings was put together by M. S. Deshpande, and first published in India in 1971. The editor was well aware of his author's dual significance, that the discoverer of satyagraha was only a persona—a disguise—for the explorer who came face to face with his God after years of struggle.

Not that in that struggle, of which tantalizing glimpses appear in this book, he started from behind. Gandhi made a statement in 1939 that reveals what spiritual advantages he began with despite growing up in a very Western-dominated India. "I learnt to rely consciously on God before I was fifteen years old." Gandhi is not referring here to formal worship, which did not play a major role in his family's life, but to the indigenous spiritualities that still obtained in those days all over India, even urban India. He refers to the piety of his mother in particular, and, above all, to that special gift which his childhood nurse give him—his mantram, the name of God, Rama, which she told him to repeat whenever he was frightened.

The child Mohandas was frightened a lot. God has a way of turning disadvantages to good. His many fears became like little hammers, pounding the tent stakes of devotion ever more firmly into the ground of his consciousness. Through Ramanama, the repetition of God's name, he erected a pavilion of such security that, as he says in this book, "The atom bomb is as nothing compared with it. This power is capable of removing all pain."

Most scholars feel today that the period of time from 1902, when he returned for a second time to South Africa, up until the successful conclusion of satyagraha there twelve years later, was his most intense period of spiritual discipline. In 1906 he learned to recognize what he called "the inner voice," and from

THE WAY TO GOD

that time on, as he says, he did not have, nor did he
need any "new experience." It is interesting to compare
this to the "kitchen epiphany" of Martin Luther King,
Jr. that took place in Montgomery, Alabama, in 1956,
the first year of the Montgomery bus boycott. Awakened by a particularly vicious phone call in the middle
of the night, he had an extreme crisis of doubt. King sat
up in his kitchen, he tells us, and prayed over an
untouched cup of coffee. "Lord, I'm down here trying to do what's right.... But Lord, I must confess that
I'm weak now. I'm faltering. I'm losing my courage."
The voice he heard then, assuring him unmistakably
that he would go forward "never alone, no, never alone,"
stayed his course for the rest of his life. Tragically, that
was to be only twelve years; for Gandhi it was to be
forty-two harrowing years of turmoil and extreme danger through which the assuring voice would guide him.

A few words about Hindu categories may help throw
into relief how Gandhi, who may have looked like a
mere politician to most westerners, was recognized by
most Indians fairly early on as a Mahatma, or Great
One. According to the Bhagavad Gita, there are three
main paths to God-realization. *Jñana,* which I would
translate as intuitive discrimination of the real amid
the changing unrealities of the phenomenal world; *bhakti,*
or self-surrender in utter love to the highest; and *karma*
or selfless work, service without personal attachment
to its fruits.

Each of these three paths, as it happens, has been embodied by a spiritual giant within the last century or more in India: *jñana* by Sri Ramana Maharshi, an immensely inspiring "knower" of pure reality who passed away in 1950 at his ashram in South India; *bhakti* by no less a figure than Sri Ramakrishna (1836–1886), whose ecstatic love of the Divine Mother and other forms of God—including Jesus and Mohammed—was so hair-trigger that he would pass into mystical states at the mere mention of a holy name; and *karma* by a failed lawyer named Mohandas Karamchand Gandhi, who, after putting himself through severe disciplines while fighting for the rights of the Indian community in South Africa, reached such a pitch of selfless activism that he worked fifteen hours a day, seven days a week, for fifty years—and owned nothing that the poorest Indian peasant could call his own.

In other words, Gandhi was a man of God of a specific type which few Indians could fail to recognize, despite its rarity. He was a *karma yogi*, and in being such became a supreme representative of what God-possession has come to mean in the otherwise godless twentieth century. This is an age of action. Wrong action is killing us, and right action alone will save us; and right action is selfless action—choosing a right goal and working tirelessly toward it with right means, and then not clinging personally to the results.

This is not to suggest that the three paths are watertight compartments. In fact there is a fourth yoga, or path, called raja, or royal yoga, in which one combines the others based on the practice of meditation. (Sri Aurobindo, who also passed away in 1950, might be its paramount exemplar in this time frame.) Gandhi was action incarnate; but his wisdom and devotion breathe forth from every page.

My own awakening to Gandhi came from my spiritual teacher, Sri Eknath Easwaran, whom I met in the fall of 1967, before he had written *Gandhi the Man*. One of the earliest books I picked up when, under his influence, my tastes and capacities began to change was the collection of Gandhi quotes *All Men Are Brothers*. I can remember the very spot where I sat thirty years ago (I'm only sitting a hundred yards or so from there now) as its wisdom rolled over me in aphorism after aphorism, addressing everything I needed wisdom about, from sex to selfless action. For me, the present book is comparable, and its great strength is that it deals with the heart of the Mahatma, his spirituality, while hinting at the many directions in which his spiritual power sent its healing influence in the world.

Take, for example, "True faith is appropriation of the reasoned experience of people whom we believe to have lived a life purified by prayer and penance." This is Gandhi at his best, at the edge of the envelope that borders human understanding in its normal modes, peering into the depths of his own experience, seeing past a contradiction that bedevils most of us, in this case the "contradiction" between faith and reason. I often think that no one enjoyed using his intellect more than Gandhi; but no one moved so easily beyond it.

Hinduism, or rather the ancient philosophical background from which Hinduism and other Indian faiths emerge, has had many glorious achievements. Several are right here in this succinct definition of faith. The first we might mention is that this time-tested system of thought, sometimes called simply the Vedanta, sets up no wall between religion and science. No Indian Galileo was forced to recant his heresies. Truth is truth. You can find it in the outside world, where we in the West have located what we like to call science, and you can find it in the world within, where—if we still believe there is such a world—we confine religion. But they are different ways of looking at reality, not different realities.

Gandhi is also suggesting here that the world beyond our senses has laws which we can vaguely discern, experiment with, eventually rely on. In this process we need all the help we can get. We need a reasonable hypothesis, "some working assumptions," as he says in this book; we need the honesty to reject those assumptions when experience contradicts them, and we need guidance from those who have gone on before us.

Two other foundation stones of the Vedanta now come into play. Spirituality is not so much taught, they say, as caught. That is, it does not drop out of the sky any more than we can think our way into it with our shaky intellects. We catch it from one another. And, second, the Great Ones who are there for us in this way have become what they are as a result of a lot of work; they are "purified by much prayer and penance." No one becomes qualified to teach this wisdom by mere charisma or self-appointment (a danger which the "New Age" doesn't always avoid). They performed often grueling disciplines—for example, Gandhi's own dogged repetition of the mantram, and his fasts and other austerities. In this connection, we might compare a Western definition of faith which is equally brilliant in its way, that of Simone Weil. "Faith is the submission of that part of the mind which has not seen God to the part which has." Gandhi would have loved that—but at the same time, his tradition gave him a deep reverence for the Great Ones who come into our life to guide and nourish us even in our most intimate struggles.

Another great achievement of the Vedanta will appear in these pages, for at several points we see Gandhi's characteristic location of his personal faith within a universe of possibilities. "There are innumerable definitions of God ... but I worship God as truth only." "Though my reason and heart long ago realized the highest attribute and name of God as truth, I recognize truth by the name of Rama." Not "This is the way," but "This is my way even though I honor yours." How badly we need this wisdom now.

But perhaps what Gandhi would have wanted himself, and what many people who turn to Gandhi today

are actually seeking, is not so much these gems of wisdom, exhilarating as they are, but practical tips from
his vast experiments in every compartment of life, from
health care to revolutions, and, in particular, practical
tips on the art of living spiritually in the world. Part
Three, Spiritual Practice, is thus where the present
selection really comes into its own, particularly its brief
section, chapter ten, on the complementary practices
of meditation and Ramanama.

Gandhi laid greater emphasis on the latter; in fact,
he hardly mentioned meditation by name in all his writings. This is probably because using a short, hallowed
formula or name of God silently in one's mind can be
done by anyone, in many common situations. On the
other hand, the regular practice of meditation for set
periods, wrestling the mind down to no distractions at
all, while in theory available to absolutely anyone, is in
practice so difficult and so unsupported by our surroundings as to be immensely difficult and still only
taken up by rare individuals, even in India. For someone with an intensely devotional nature, like Gandhi,
repeating a mantram can take one all the way—that
is, if one keeps at it with the intensity Gandhi describes
in these pages. For others, the practice of Ramanama,
chanted silently to oneself, or sung out loud in groups,
a practice which has been hit upon in every major religion, is still immensely helpful.

When you appreciate how utterly, through repetition of his mantram, Gandhi conquered fear, so that

the most embattled empire the world had ever seen could not cow him, when you realize that he died with name of Rama on his lips, you realize that this nurse Rambha, about whom the historical record is so silent, was one of the most important figures of the twentieth century. She catalyzed the making of the Mahatma.

If Ramanama is the most appealing of Gandhi's spiritual suggestions, it would be cowardly of us not to say a few words about what is bound to be the least attractive, the dreaded brahmacharya, or celibacy. Deshpande titles this section rather bluntly, Conquest of Lust, and that may be exactly the problem in this age—who wants to conquer it?

Actually, brahmacharya (literally, God-conduct) means both more and less than sexual abstinence. It means more because it stands for control over all sense experience. Gandhi is perfectly clear that not having sex while indulging in everything else one likes is as useful as building a dam halfway across a river. Brahmacharya is also more than sexual abstinence because it is intended to apply not merely to our behavior, but to the roots of behavior, to control over our words and, in the end, over our very thoughts. As Jesus and Gandhi believe, when we lust after someone, or something, in our heart, the damage is already done. So brahmacharya is a very tall order indeed.

At the same time, it is less than, or at least different from, a total ban on sense pleasures. That is not how we are to think of it at all. To begin with, Gandhi makes quite clear, in the present collection and elsewhere, that brahmacharya has almost nothing to do with morality. It is an engineering issue—what do you want to do with your vital energy? This is one of the key questions of human life, and one that for many of us is no longer well addressed through the categories of good and evil. Ultimately, it is a question of power; and ultimately, "All power comes from the observation and sublimation of the vitality that is responsible for the creation of life."

We can be confident that the moralistic vocabulary Gandhi used writing for an Indian audience in midcentury would not be the vocabulary he would use if, by some miracle, he were able to address turn-of-the-century America. For them he said, "The palate is the chief sinner." For us he might say, as he did elsewhere, "The control of the palate is a valuable aid in the control of the mind." It is in this framework that we should approach the struggle to come to grips with all the vagaries of our mind, and that struggle is most acute where the life-force is most intimately involved—in the power given to man and woman to create new life.

We can perhaps illustrate this connection with an episode from Gandhi's own experience. In the summer of 1906, Gandhi was doing ambulance service in South Africa in what was known as "the Zulu Rebellion." What he went through in this carnage, which was actually a massacre of Zulus by the well-armed whites, we can only imagine. But for some reason the crisis brought him to a personal decision that was to set his course irrevocably for the rest of his life.

> During the difficult marches that had then to be performed, the idea flashed upon me that, if I wanted to devote myself to the service of the community in this manner, I must relinquish the desire for children and wealth and live the life of a *vanaprastha*—of one retired from household cares.

When this idea "flashed upon" the soon-to-be Mahatma, it was translated into immediate action. He meant that he would, and he did, renounce all possessions and renounce sexual practice from that time on. He was thirty-seven. His four sons were born. He would be as good a husband and father as the immense demands on him would allow, but he would no more live for self and immediate family from that moment.

Barely three months later, on September 11, 1906, in the Empire Jewish Theater of Johannesburg, the Indian community responded to his leadership and vowed "with God as their witness" that they would never obey the discriminatory legislation about to be passed against them by the Transvaal parliament. At this moment satyagraha was born. I do not think this is a coincidence. The terrific renunciation lead immediately to a lifetime opportunity—and the courage to recognize and seize it. Though he never mentions this particular connection, it is a clear enough subtext in both his *Satyagraha in South Africa* and his *Autobiography.* The general principle is explicitly clear even in this collection: we have to make a choice in life whether to serve others or serve only ourselves. Again, it is not a moral choice but, if you will, a matter of investment. In his case that choice was all-or-nothing. He claims that it made him supremely happy, almost from the outset. "I realized that a vow, far from closing the door to real freedom, opened it." The struggle gave him an unending joy which, he later said, "I have no power to describe."

There are two things we should bear in mind if we want to understand the point of a self-imposed discipline like brahmacharya. The first is that it is just that, self-imposed. "Restraint self-imposed is not compulsion." These are not restraints imposed from anyone else, or by society or religion. They are experiments imposed on the self by the self. They are undertaken in freedom and they lead to freedom. Gandhi felt it would actually be wrong to do them because someone else tells us to.

Second, this is not about depriving ourselves of satisfaction. It's about choosing what kind of satisfaction to invest in. Shall we use the endowment of vital energy we've been given for experiences that give pleasure, of which sex is paramount for almost all people, or shall we use that same endowment for what we consider higher ends? What we often forget to include in the equation is the fact that higher ends bring higher satisfactions—even if they are not as vividly present to us at the moment. Shall we use it, in the terms of this little book, to get to God?

In Part Four, Spiritual Experience, *The Way to God* closes with a dramatic flourish. Gandhi describes hearing the voice of God. If it were anyone else, we might dismiss what he tells us as imaginary. But Gandhi's dedication to truth is so unswerving that it's difficult to accept that he would permit himself even to exaggerate in a matter so important. How else, in any case, can we explain the vast impact of this event? In September, 1932, Gandhi undertook what history knows as his "Epic Fast." As a result, many of the most sacred temples of India were opened, for the first time, to the underclass of untouchables.

Six months later, the voice of God came to him. It urged him to fast again, this time for twenty-one days, to complete the self-purification needed to conquer class injustice in India. Friends from around the world came to his support. The Hindu community of India watched the Mahatma's decline, and when the fast ended, caste prejudice had been dealt a stunning blow, its legitimacy and religious aura crippled forever.

Not that Gandhi himself is overly concerned whether we believe him about the voice. We are "free to say that it was all self-delusion or hallucination." But "not the unanimous verdict of the whole world" could shake him from the belief that this was indeed God's voice. Elsewhere he explains that he does not make such claims for himself only. It is open to everyone. "Here is no question of hallucination. I have described a simple, scientific law which can be verified by all those who will develop the necessary qualifications; which are, again, incredibly simple to understand and easy enough to follow if one has the determination." Gandhi so rarely mentioned his inner experiences that we treasure this revelation.

In their *Essays in Gandhian Economics*, editors Romesh Diwan and Mark Lutz muse,

> Looking back, one is amazed at the acute understanding of each of the problems by Mahatma Gandhi. He dealt with some problems more intensively than others but he never lost sight of any one of them. He denounced the concept of an economic man because he refused to recognize the separation of economics from ethics. He denounced the technological determinism because it enslaved man and sanctified only those technologies that conformed to value premises. Above all, he struggled against the mightiest imperial power in terms of nonviolent theory and order. As he went along with these tasks, he discovered his own science of Economics.

Similarly, today, contemplating the horrors of modern, post-industrial colonialism, whose lust to exploit reaches into the very code of nature, into genes and seeds, Indian ecologist and physicist Vandana Shiva declares that Gandhi's "is the most important philosophy in our times.... There is no other philosophy that can get people out of our current crisis."

How can one person have been so sagacious? I submit that the answer lies in this little book. Gandhi went to the heart of everything and touched the heart of millions because he chose and clung to the one essential thing, which is to awaken God or truth within the individual.

Never think for a moment that this is a selfish, narcissistic endeavor. He realized as early as 1909, while steaming to India on board the S.S. Kildonan Castle and composing his tractate *Indian Home Rule*, that we are caught in a struggle, not between two peoples or two nations but between two ways of life. St. Augustine, in *City of God*, had called them two cities growing respectively out of two human loves—the love of self, or the love of the larger whole that Augustine called God. Right now the city of man, the culture of self-love and greed, seems out of control. Call it what you will, Gandhi's way to God is the way to that other city of love and justice.

The Way to God

I know the path. It is straight and narrow. It is sharp as a razor. I rejoice to walk on it. When I slip, I weep. God's word is, he who strives never perishes. I have implicit faith in that promise. Though, therefore, from my weakness, I fail a thousand times, I will not lose faith.

I would like to say to the diligent reader of my writings, and to others who are interested in them, that I am not at all concerned with appearing to be consistent. . . . What I am concerned with is my readiness to obey the call of truth, my God, from moment to moment, and therefore, when anybody finds any inconsistency between any two writings of mine, if he has still faith in my sanity, he would do well to choose the later of the two on the same subject.

Part One
Intellectual Foundation

God

1. God Is One, Without a Second

God is certainly one. He has no second. He is unfathomable, unknowable and unknown to the vast majority of mankind. He is everywhere. He sees without eyes and hears without ears. He is formless and indivisible. He is uncreate, has no father, mother, or child; and yet he allows himself to be worshipped as father, mother, wife, and child. He allows himself even to be worshipped as stock and stone, although he is none of these things. He is the most elusive. He is the nearest to us, if we would but know the fact. But he is farthest from us when we do not want to realize his omnipresence.

I dispute the description that Hindus believe in many gods and are idolaters. They do say that there are many gods, but they also declare unmistakably that there is one god, the god of gods. It is not, therefore, proper to suggest that Hindus believe in many gods. They certainly believe in many worlds. Just as there is a world inhabited by men and another by beast, so also, is there one inhabited by superior beings called gods, whom we do not see but who nevertheless exist. The whole mischief is created by the English rendering of the word *deva* or *devata*, for which you have not found a better term than "god." But God is Ishwara, Devadhideva, god of gods. So you see it is the word "god" used to describe different divine beings that has given rise to such confusion. I believe that I am a thorough Hindu but I never believe in many gods. Never even in my childhood did I hold that belief and no one ever taught me to do so.

2. He Is Omnipresent, Omniscient, and Omnipotent

God is not some person outside ourselves or away from the universe. He pervades everything and is omniscient as well as omnipotent. He does not need any praise or petitions. Being immanent in all beings, he hears everything and reads our innermost thoughts. He abides in our hearts and is nearer to us than the nails on our fingers.

God is then not a person. He is the all-pervading, all-powerful spirit. Anyone who hears him in his heart has accession of a marvelous force or energy, comparable in its results to physical forces like steam or electricity but much more subtle.

3. He Is a Mysterious Power

There is an indefinable mysterious power that pervades everything. I feel it though I don't see it. It is this unseen power which makes itself felt and yet defies all proof, because it is so unlike all that I perceive through my senses. It transcends the senses.

I do dimly perceive that whilst everything around me is ever changing and ever dying, there is underlying all that change a living power that is changeless, that holds all together, that creates, dissolves, and recreates. This informing power or spirit is God.

The truth is that God is the force. He is the essence of life. He is pure, undefiled consciousness. He is eternal. And yet, strangely enough, all are not able to derive either benefit from, or shelter in, the all-pervading living presence.

Electricity is a powerful force. Not all can benefit from it. It can only be produced by following certain laws. It is a lifeless force. Man can utilize it if he can labor hard enough to acquire the knowledge of its laws. The living force which we call God can similarly be followed if we know and follow his law leading to the discovery of him in us.

God is an unseen power residing within us. There are many powers lying hidden within us and we discover them by constant struggle. Even so, we may find this supreme power if we make diligent search with the fixed determination to find him.

My God does not reside above. He has to be realized

on earth. He is here, within you, within me. He is omnipotent and omnipresent. You need not think of the world beyond. If we can do our duty here, the beyond will take care of itself.

4. The Supreme Good

Is this power benevolent or malevolent? I see it as purely benevolent. For I can see that in the midst of death, life persists; in the midst of untruth, truth persists; in the midst of darkness, light persists. Hence, I gather that God is life, truth, light. He is love. He is the supreme good.

God is wholly good. There is no evil in him. God made man in his own image. Unfortunately for us, man has fashioned him in his own. This arrogation has landed mankind in a sea of troubles. God is the supreme alchemist. In his presence all iron and dross turn into pure gold. Similarly does all evil turn into good.

Again God lives, but not as we. His creatures live but to die. But God is life. Therefore, goodness and all it connotes is not an attribute. Goodness is God. Goodness conceived as apart from him is a lifeless thing.... So are all morals. If they are to live in us, they must be considered and cultivated in their relation to God. We try to become good, because we want to reach and realize God. All the dry ethics of the world turns to dust because apart from God they are lifeless. Coming from God they come with life in them. They become part of us and ennoble us.

5. God Is Truth and Love

The absolute truth, the eternal principle, that is God. There are innumerable definitions of God, because his manifestations are innumerable. They overwhelm me with wonder and awe and for a moment stun me. But I worship God as truth only.

To me God is truth and love. God is ethics and morality; God is fearlessness. God is the source of light and life, and yet he is above and beyond all these. God is conscience. He is even the atheism of the atheist. For in his boundless love, God permits the atheist to live. He is the searcher of the hearts. He knows us and our hearts better than we do ourselves.... He is personal god to those who need his personal presence. He is embodied to those who need his touch. He is the purest essence. He is, to those who have faith. He is all things to all men.

6. God Is Sat-Chit-Ananda

Truth, knowledge, Bliss

The word *satya*, truth, is derived from *sat* which means being. And nothing is or exists in reality except truth. That is why *Sat*, or truth, is perhaps the most important name of God. In fact, it is more correct to say truth is

God than to say God is truth.

And where there is truth, there is also knowledge, which is true. Where there is no truth, there can be no true knowledge. That is why the word *chit*, or knowledge, is associated with the name of God.

And where there is true knowledge, there is always bliss, *ananda*. Sorrow has no place there. And even as truth is eternal, so is the Bliss derived from it. Hence we know God as *Sat-Chit-Ananda*, one who combines in himself truth, knowledge, and bliss.

7. He Is Law Eternal

God is an idea, Law himself.... He and his law abide everywhere and govern everything. Therefore, though I do not think that he answers, in every detail, every request of ours, there is no doubt that he rules our actions, and I literally believe that not a blade of grass grows or moves without his will.

I do feel that there is orderliness in the universe, that there is an unalterable law governing everything and every being that lives and moves. It is not a blind law, for no blind law can govern the conduct of living beings.... The law and the lawgiver are one. I may not deny the law or lawgiver, because I know so little about it or him. Even as my denial or ignorance of the existence of an earthly power will avail nothing, so will not my denial of God and his law liberate me from its operation; whereas, humble and mute acceptance of divine authority makes life's journey easier, even as acceptance of earthly rule makes life under it easier.

8. His Infinite Mercy

God is, even though the whole world deny him. God embraces not only this tiny globe of ours, but millions and billions of such globes. How can we—little crawling creatures so utterly helpless as he has made us—how could we possibly measure his greatness, his boundless love, his infinite compassion? So great is his infinite love and pity that he allows man insolently to deny him, wrangle about him, and cut the throats of his fellow men. How can we measure the greatness of God, who is so forgiving, so divine?

He allows us freedom and yet his compassion commands obedience to his will. But if anyone of us disdains to bow to his will, he says, "So be it. My sun will shine no less for thee. My clouds will rain no less for thee. I need not force thee to accept my sway." Of such a God let the ignorant dispute the existence. I am one of the millions of wise men who believe in him and am never tired of bowing to him and singing his glory.

God is the hardest taskmaster I have known on earth. He tries you through and through. And when you find your faith is failing, or your body is failing you and you are sinking, he comes to your assistance somehow or other and proves to you that you must not lose your faith, and that he is always at your beck and call, but on his terms. So I have found. I cannot recall a single instance when, at the eleventh hour, he has forsaken me.

9. He Has Many Names

There is only one omnipotent and omnipresent God. He is named variously and we remember him by the name which is most familiar to us. Each person can choose the name that appeals most to him. Ishwara, Allah, Khuda, God mean the same.

God has a thousand names, or rather, he is nameless. We may worship or pray to him by whichever name that pleases us. All worship the same spirit, but as all foods do not agree with all, all names do not appeal to all. Each chooses the name according to his associations, and he being the indweller, all-powerful and omniscient, knows our inmost feelings and responds to us according to our deserts.

In my opinion, Rama, Rahaman, Ahurmazda, God, or Krishna, are all attempts on the part of man to name that invisible force.... Man can only conceive God within the limitations of his own mind. What matters, then, whether one man worships God as a person and another as force? Both do right according to their lights. One need only remember that God is the force among all the forces. All other forces are material. But God is the vital force or spirit, which is all-pervading, all-embracing, and therefore beyond human ken.

Daridranarayan is one of millions of names by which humanity knows God who is unnameable and unfathomable by human understanding. And it means, God of the poor, God appearing in the hearts of the poor.

10. His Incarnations

God is not a person. To affirm that he descends to earth every now and again in the form of a human being is a partial truth, which merely signifies that such a person lives near to God. Inasmuch as God is omnipresent, he dwells within every human being and all may, therefore, be said to be incarnations of him. But this leads us nowhere. Rama, Krishna, etc., are called incarnations of God because we attribute divine qualities to them. Whether they actually lived or not does not affect the picture of them in man's mind.

Soul

1. Spark of Divinity

We may not be God, but we are of God, even as a little drop of water is of the ocean. Imagine it torn away from the ocean and flung millions of miles away. It becomes helpless, torn from its surroundings, and cannot feel the might and majesty of the ocean. But if some one could point out to it that it is the ocean, its faith would revive, it would dance with joy and the whole of the might and majesty of the ocean would be reflected in it.

2. Man Is the Image of God

Man alone is made in the image of God. That some of us do not recognize that status of ours, makes no difference, except that we do not get the benefit of the status, even as a lion brought up in the company of sheep may not know his own status, and therefore does not receive its benefits. But it belongs to him, nevertheless, and the moment he realizes it, he begins to exercise his dominion over the sheep. But no sheep masquerading as a lion can ever attain the leonine status. And to prove the proposition that man is made in the image of God, it is unnecessary to show that all men admittedly exhibit that image in their own person. It is enough to show that one man at least has done so. And will it be denied that the great religious teachers of mankind have exhibited the image of God in their persons?

3. Life Is a Mere Bubble

Our existence as embodied beings is purely momentary. What are a hundred years in eternity? But if we shatter the chains of egotism, and melt into the ocean of humanity, we share its dignity. To feel that we are something is to set up a barrier between God and ourselves. To cease feeling that we are something is to become one with God. A drop in the ocean partakes of the greatness of its parent, although it is unconscious of it. But it is dried up as soon as it enters upon an existence independent of the ocean. We do not exaggerate when we say that life is a bubble.

4. Life and Death

It is as clear to me as daylight that life and death are but phases of the same thing, the reverse and obverse of the same coin. In fact, tribulation and death seem to me to present a phase far richer than happiness or life. What is life worth without trials and tribulations, which are the salt of life? ... I want you all to treasure death and suffering more than life, and to appreciate their cleansing and purifying character.

The body must suffer for its ill deeds. We die to live once more, even as we live to die at last. Life, therefore, is not an occasion for joy, nor is death an occasion for sorrow. But there is one thing needful. We must ascertain our duty in life and continue to discharge it till we die.

Death is at any time blessed, but it is twice blessed for a warrior who dies for his cause, i.e. truth. Death is no fiend, he is the truest of friends. He delivers us from agony. He helps us against ourselves. He ever gives us new chances, new hopes. He is like a sleep, a sweet restorer. Yet it is customary to mourn when a friend dies. The custom has no operation when the death is that of a martyr.

5. Freedom of Choice

Man has reason, discrimination, and free will such as it is. The brute has no such thing. It is not a free agent and knows no distinction between virtue and vice, good and evil. Man, being a free agent, knows these distinctions and when he follows his higher nature, shows himself far superior to the brute, but when he follows his baser nature, can show himself lower than the brute.

But this free will we enjoy is less than that of a passenger on a crowded deck. Man is the maker of his own destiny in the sense that he has freedom of choice as to the manner in which he uses his freedom. But he is no controller of results. The moment he thinks he is, he comes to grief.

It is man's special privilege and pride to be gifted with the faculties of head and heart both, that he is a thinking no less than a feeling animal. . . . In man reason quickens and guides the feeling. In brute the soul lies dormant. To awaken the heart is to awaken the dormant soul, to awaken reason is to inculcate discrimination between good and evil.

6. Man's Primary Duty

It is the duty of every human being to look carefully within and see himself as he is, and spare no pains to improve himself in body, mind, and soul. He should realize the mischief wrought by injustice, wickedness, vanity, and the like, and do his best to fight them.

Man's estate is one of probation. During that period he is played upon by evil forces as well as good. He is ever prey to temptations. He has to prove his manliness by resisting and fighting temptations. He is no warrior who fights outside foes of his imagination and is powerless to lift his little finger against innumerable foes within or what is worse, mistakes them for friends.

It is not man's duty to develop all his faculties to perfection. His duty is to develop all his godward faculties to perfection and to suppress completely those of
contrary tendencies.

It is inherent in man, imperfect though he is, cease-
lessly to strive after perfection. In the attempt he falls
into reverie. And just as a child tries to stand, falls down
again and again, and ultimately learns how to walk,
even so, man, with all his intelligence, is a mere infant
as compared to the infinite and ageless God.

The goal ever recedes from us. The greater the progress
the greater the recognition of our unworthiness. Satisfaction lies in the effort, not in the attainment. Full
effort is full victory.

World

1. The World Is One Body

God has so ordered this world that no one can keep his goodness or badness exclusively to himself. The whole world is like the human body with its various members. Pain in one member is felt in the whole body. Rot in one part must inevitably poison the whole system. Let us, therefore, cease to think in terms of the whole country. We must put faith in God and be careful for nothing. We hold our destiny in our own hands and no one but ourselves can make or mar it.

2. The Universe: A Family of Nations

Nations cohere because there is mutual regard among the individuals composing them. Some day we must extend the nation law to the universe, even as we have extended the family law to form nations—a larger family. God has ordained that India should be such a nation.

Indeed, Hinduism teaches us to regard the whole humanity as one indivisible undivided family.

3. The Problem of Evil

Why is there evil in the world, is a difficult question to answer. I can only give what I may call a villager's answer. If there is good, there must also be evil, just as where there is light there is also darkness. But it is true only so far as we human mortals are concerned. Before God there is nothing good, nothing evil. We may talk of his dispensation in human terms, but our language is not God's.

I cannot account for the existence of evil by any rational method. To want to do so is to be coequal with God. I am therefore humble enough to recognize evil as such. And I call God long suffering and patient precisely because he permits evil in the world. I know that there is no evil in him, and yet if there is evil, he is the author of it and yet untouched by it.

4. A Pair of Opposite Forces

The distinction between good and evil thoughts is not unimportant. Nor do these thoughts come haphazard. They follow some law, which the scriptures have tried to enunciate. There are certain problems in mathematics, for the solution of which some workable assumptions have to be made. They help the solution of the problem. But they are purely imaginary, and have no other practical use. Similarly, psychologists have proceeded upon the assumption that a pair of opposite forces is warring against each other in the universe, of which one is divine and the other is devilish. The distinction is made by all the scriptures of the world. I say this distinction is imaginary. God is one, without a second. He alone is. He is indefinable. In reality there is no war between God and Satan.

5. God's Hand Is Behind Good and Evil

In a strictly scientific sense, God is at the bottom of both good and evil. He directs the assassin's dagger no less than the surgeon's knife. But for all that, good and evil are, for human purposes, from each other distinct and incompatible, being symbolical of light and darkness, God and Satan ... respectively.

God's hand is behind good, but in God's hand it is not mere good. His hand is behind evil also, but there it is no longer evil. "Good" and "Evil" is our own imperfect language. God is above both good and evil.

It is we who entertain thoughts, and it is we ourselves who repulse them. We have, thus, to strive against ourselves. The scriptures have, therefore, said that there is a duel in the world. This duel is imaginary, not real. We can, however, sustain ourselves in the world by assuming the existence of the imaginary duel to be real.

6. Blessings of Calamity

It is the universal experience that every calamity brings a sensible man down on his knees. He thinks that it is God's answer to his sins and that he must henceforth behave better. His sins have left him hopelessly weak, and in his weakness he cried out to God for help. Thus millions of human beings used their personal calamities for self-improvement. Nations too have been known to invoke the assistance of God when calamities have overtaken them. They have abased themselves before God and appointed days of humiliation, prayer, and purification.

Part Two
Moral Discipline

Truth

1. What Is Truth?

What is truth? A difficult question, but I have solved it for myself, by saying that it is what the voice within tells you. How then, you ask, do different people think of different and contrary truths?

It is because we have at the present moment everybody claiming the right of conscience without going through any discipline whatsoever; there is so much untruth being delivered in a bewildered world. All that I can, in true humility, present to you is that truth is not to be found by anybody who has not got an abundant sense of humility. If you would swim on the bosom of the ocean of truth, you must reduce yourself to a zero.

Truth is within ourselves. There is an inmost center in us all, where truth abides in fullness. Every wrongdoer knows within himself that he is doing wrong, for untruth cannot be mistaken for truth. Truth and righteousness must for ever remain the law in God's world.

The law of truth is merely understood to mean that we must speak the truth. But we understand the word in a much wider sense. There should be truth in thought, truth in speech, and truth in action.

2. Truth Is the Source of Character

Character is based on virtuous action, and virtuous action is grounded on truth. Truth, then, is the source and foundation of all things that are good and great. Hence fearless and unflinching pursuit of the ideal of truth and righteousness is the key of true health, as of all else.

3. How to Realize Truth

But how is one to realize truth, which may be likened to the philosopher's stone or the cow of plenty? By single-minded devotion, *abhyasa*, and indifference to every other interest, *vairagya*.

Silence is a great help to a seeker after truth like myself. In the attitude of silence, the soul finds the path in clearer light, and what is elusive and deceptive resolves itself into crystal clearness. Our life is a long arduous quest after truth, and the soul requires inward restfulness to attain its full height.

Experience has taught me that silence is a part of the spiritual discipline of a votary of truth. Proneness to exaggerate, to suppress, or to modify truth, wittingly or unwittingly, is a natural weakness of man, and silence is necessary in order to surmount it. A man of few words will rarely be thoughtless in his speech. He will measure every word.

4. The Need for Fearless Vigilance

There is so much superstition and hypocrisy around, that one is afraid even to do the right thing. But if one gives way to fear, even truth will have to be suppressed. The golden rule is to act fearlessly upon what one believes to be right.... The danger is that when we are surrounded by falsehood on all sides, we might be caught in it and begin to deceive ourselves. We should be careful not to make a mistake, out of our laziness and ignorance. Constant vigilance under all circumstances is essential.

5. Its Supreme Value

How beautiful it would be if all of us, young and old, men and women, devoted ourselves wholly to truth in all that we might do—in our waking hours, whether working, eating, drinking, or playing, till pure dreamless sleep claimed us for her own. God as truth has been for me a treasure beyond price. May he be so to every one of us!

Therefore, the pursuit of truth is true *bhakti*. It is the path that leads to God. There is no place in it for cowardice, no place for defeat. It is the talisman by which death itself becomes the portal to life eternal.

Love

1. Truth and Love

Love and truth are faces of the same coin, and both
very difficult to practice, and the only things worth living for. A person cannot be true if he does not love all
God's creatures. Truth and love are therefore the complete sacrifice. Without truth there is no love. Without
truth it may be affection, as for one's country, to the
injury of others; or infatuation, as of a young man for
a girl.... Love transcends all animality and is never
partial.

   True love is boundless like the ocean and, swelling
within one, spreads itself out and, crossing all bound-
aries and frontiers, envelops the whole world.

2. Love Unites

Scientists tell us that without the presence of the cohesive force amongst atoms that comprise the globe of
ours, it would crumble to pieces and we would cease
to exist; and even as there is a cohesive force in blind
matter, so must there be in all things animate, and the
name for that cohesive force among animate beings is
love. We notice it between father and son, between

brother and sister, friend and friend. But we have to learn to use that force among all that lives. In the use of it consists our knowledge of God.

3. Love Is Life

If love was not the law of life, life would not have persisted in the midst of death. Life is a perpetual triumph over the grave. If there is a fundamental distinction between man and beast, it is the former's progressive recognition of the law and its application in practice to his own personal life. All the saints of the world, ancient and modern, were each, according to his light and capacity, a living illustration of that supreme law of our being. That the brute in us seems so often to gain easy triumph, is true enough. How should it be otherwise with a law which is as high as truth itself? When the practice of the law becomes universal, God will reign on earth as he does in Heaven. . . . I need not be reminded that earth and Heaven are within us. We know the earth, we are strangers to Heaven within us.

It is my firm belief that it is love that sustains the earth. There only is life where there is love. Life without love is death. Love is the reverse of the coin of which the obverse is truth.

Hatred ever kills; love never dies. Such is the vast difference between the two. What is obtained by love is retained for all time. What is obtained by hatred proves a burden in reality, for it increases hatred. The duty of a human being is to diminish hatred and to promote love.

4. The Law of Love

The law of love, call it attraction, affinity, cohesion if you like, governs the world. The universe continues in spite of destruction incessantly going on. Truth triumphs over untruth. Love conquers hatred. God eternally triumphs over Satan.

We will have ample cause to congratulate ourselves if we learn to substitute the law of love in society for that of the jungle, and instead of harboring ill will and enmity in our bosoms against those whom we regard as our enemies, we learn to love them, as actual and potential friends.

5. The Religion of Ahimsa

The world is full of violence, *himsa,* and nature does appear to be "red in tooth and claw." But if we bear in mind that the man is higher than the brute, then is man superior to nature. If man has a divine mission to fulfill, a mission that becomes him, it is that of nonviolence, *ahimsa.*

I am not a visionary. I claim to be a practical idealist. The religion of nonviolence is not meant merely for rishis and saints. It is meant for the common people as well. Nonviolence is the law of our species, as violence is the law of the brute. The dignity of man requires obedience to such a higher law to strengthen the spirit.

Man as animal is violent, but as a spirit is nonviolent. The moment he awakes to the spirit within, he cannot remain violent. Either he progresses towards ahimsa, or rushes towards his doom. That is why the prophets and the avatars have taught the lesson of truth, harmony, brotherhood, justice, etc., all attributes of *ahimsa.*

So let no one doubt that the salvation of all the exploited peoples of the earth, and therefore of the world, lies in the strictest reliance on the coin on whose one face is written "truth," and on the other "nonviolence," in large letters. Sixty years of experience has taught me no other method.

Self-Restraint

1. Restraint Should Be Voluntary

Restraint self-imposed is not compulsion. A man who chooses the path of freedom from restraint, i.e. self-indulgence, will be a bond slave of passions, whilst a man who binds himself to rules and restraints releases himself. All things in the universe, including the sun and the moon and the stars, obey certain laws. Without the restraining influence of these laws, the world would not go on for a single moment.... It is discipline and restraint that separates us from the brute. If we would be men walking with our heads erect and not walking on all fours, let us understand and put ourselves under voluntary discipline and restraint.

2. Control of the Palate

True happiness is impossible without true health and true health is impossible without a rigid control of the palate. All the other senses will automatically come under our control when the palate has been brought under control. And he who has conquered his senses has really conquered the whole world.

One should eat not in order to please the palate but just to keep the body going. When each organ of sense subserves the body and, through the body, the soul, its specific relish disappears, and then alone does it begin to function in the way nature intended it to do. Any number of experiments is too small and no sacrifice too great for attaining this symphony with nature.

3. Conquest of Lust

The conquest of lust is the highest endeavor of man or woman's existence. Without overcoming lust man cannot hope to rule over self. And without rule over self there can be no swaraj or ramaraj. Rule of all without rule of oneself would prove to be as deceptive and disappointing as a painted toy mango, charming to look at outwardly, but hollow and empty within. . . . Great causes call for spiritual effort or soul-force. Soul-force comes only through God's grace, and God's grace never descends upon a man who is a slave to lust.

Brahmacharya means control of all organs of sense. He who attempts to control only one organ and allows all others free play is bound to find his effort futile. To hear suggestive stories with ears, to see suggestive sights with the eyes, to taste stimulating food with the tongue, to touch exciting things with the hands, and then at the same time, try to control the only remaining organ, is like putting one's hand in fire and then

trying to escape being burnt. If we practice simulta-
neous self-control in all directions, the attempt is scientific and easy of success. Perhaps the palate is the
chief sinner. Hence we have assigned to its control a
separate place among the observances.

4. Sublimation of Vitality

All power comes from the observation and sublimation of the vitality that is responsible for the creation
of life. If the vitality is husbanded instead of being
dissipated, it is transmuted into creative energy of the
highest order.... This vitality is dissipated by evil
thoughts. And since thought is the root of all speech
and action, the quality of the latter corresponds to that
of the former. Hence perfectly controlled thought is
itself a power of the highest potency and can become
self-acting.... Such power is impossible in one who
dissipates his energy, even as steam kept in a leaking
pot yields no power.

5. Restraint vs. Suppression

It is harmful to suppress the body if the mind at the
same time is allowed to go astray. Where the mind wan-
ders, the body must follow, sooner or later. It is necessary here to appreciate one distinction. It is one thing
to allow the mind to harbor impure thoughts, it is a
different thing altogether if it strays among them in

spite of ourselves. Victory will be ours in the end, if we non-cooperate with the mind in this evil process.... Hence the body must be immediately taken in hand, and then we must put forth a constant endeavor to bring the mind under control. We can do nothing more, nothing less.

Restraint never ruins one's health. What ruins one's health is not restraint, but outward suppression. A really self-restrained person grows every day from strength to strength and from peace to more peace. The very first step in self-restraint is the restraint of thoughts. Understand your limitations and do only as much as you can.... Let not what I have told you alarm you or weaken you. Always aim at complete harmony of thought and word and deed. Always aim at purifying your thoughts and everything will be well. There is nothing more potent than thought—deed follows word and word follows thought. The world is the result of a mighty thought, and where the thought is mighty and pure, the result is always mighty and pure.

Selfless Service

1. Selfless Service Is a Source of Joy

The human body is meant solely for service, never for indulgence. The secret of happy life lies in renunciation. Renunciation is life. Indulgence is death. Therefore everyone has a right, and should desire, to live 125 years while performing service without an eye on result. Such life must be wholly and solely dedicated to service. Renunciation made for the sake of service is an ineffable joy of which none can deprive one, because that nectar springs from within and sustains life. In this there can be no room for worry or impatience. Without this joy, long life is impossible and would not be worthwhile even if possible.

The soul is omnipresent. Why should she care to be confined within the cage-like body, or do evil and even kill for the sake of the cage? We thus arrive at the ideal of total renunciation, and learn to use the body for the purpose of service, so long as it exists, so much so that service and not bread becomes, with us, the staff of life. We eat and drink, sleep and awake, for service alone. Such an attitude of mind brings us real happiness and beatific vision in the fullness of time.

2. Service Is Meant for Self-Realization

I am here to serve no one else but myself, to find my own self-realization through the service of these village folk. Man's ultimate aim is the realization of God, and all his activities—social, political, religious—have to be guided by the ultimate aim of the vision of God. The immediate service of human beings becomes a necessary part of the endeavor, simply because the only way to find God is to see him in his creation and be one with it. This can only be done through one's country. I am part and parcel of the whole, and I cannot find him apart from the rest of humanity. My countrymen are my nearest neighbors. They have become so helpless, so resourceless, so inert that I must concentrate on serving them. If I could persuade myself that I should find him in a Himalayan cave, I would proceed there immediately. But I know that I cannot find him apart from humanity.

3. Service Leads to Salvation

I am striving for the Kingdom of Heaven, which is spiritual deliverance. For me the road to salvation lies through incessant toil in the service of my country and my humanity. I want to identify myself with everything that lives. In the language of the *Gita*, I want to live at peace with both friend and foe. My patriotism is for me a stage on my journey to the land of eternal free-

dom and peace. Thus it will be seen that, for me, there
are no politics devoid of religion. They subserve religion. Politics bereft of religion are a deathtrap because
they kill the soul.

4. Service Should Be Constant

A life of service must be one of humility. He who
could sacrifice his life for others has hardly time to
reserve for himself a place in the sun. Inertia must not
be mistaken for humility, as it has been in Hinduism.
True humility means most strenuous and constant
endeavor, entirely directed towards the service of
humanity. God is continuously in action without rest-
ing for a single moment. If we should serve him or
become one with him, our activity must be as unwea-
ried as his. There may be momentary rest in store for the
drop which is separated from the ocean, but not for
the drop in the ocean, which knows no rest. The same
is the case with ourselves. As soon as we become one
with the ocean in the shape of God, there is no more
rest for us, nor indeed do we need rest any longer. Our
very sleep is action. For we sleep with the thought of
God in our hearts. This restlessness constitutes true
rest. This never-ceasing agitation holds the key to peace
ineffable. This supreme state of total surrender is difficult to describe, but not beyond the bounds of human
experience. It has been attained by many dedicated
souls, and may be attained by ourselves as well.

Part Three
Spiritual Practice

Faith

1. Disbelief Is a Disease

It is the fashion, nowadays, to dismiss God from life altogether and insist on the possibility of reaching the highest kind of life without the necessity of a living faith in a living God. I must confess my inability to drive the truth of the law home to those who have no faith in, and no need for, a power infinitely higher than themselves. My own experience has led me to the knowledge that fullest life is impossible without an immovable belief in a living law, in obedience to which the whole universe moves. A man without that faith is like a drop thrown out of the ocean which is bound to perish. Every drop in the ocean shares its majesty, and has the honor of giving us the ozone of life.

It is easy enough to say, "I do not believe in God," for God permits all things to be said of him with impunity. He looks at our acts. And any breach of his law brings with it not its vindictive, but its purifying, compelling punishment. God's existence cannot be, does not need to be, proved. God is. If he is not felt, so much the worse for us. The absence of feeling is a disease which we shall some day throw off, *nolens volens*.

2. The Need for a Living Faith

No search is possible without some working assumptions. If we grant nothing we find nothing. Ever since its commencement, the world—the wise and foolish included—has proceeded on the assumption that if we are, God is, and that if God is not, we are not. And since belief in God is coexistent with humankind, existence of God is treated as a fact more definite than the fact that the sun is. This living faith has solved the largest number of puzzles of life. It has alleviated our misery. It sustains us in life; it is our solace in death.

3. Testimony of Saints

True faith is appropriation of the reasoned experience of people whom we believe to have lived a life purified by prayer and penance. Belief, therefore, in prophets and incarnations who have lived in remote ages is not an idle superstition but a satisfaction of an inmost spiritual want.

They say that anybody following the path they have trodden can realize God. The fact is, we do not want to follow the path leading to realization, and we won't take the testimony of eyewitnesses about the one thing that really matters.

4. Faith and Reason

There are subjects where reason cannot take us far and we have to accept things on faith. Faith, then, does not contradict reason but transcends it. Faith is a kind of sixth sense which works in cases which are without the purview of reason.

Faith only begins where reason stops. But there are very few actions in the world for which reasonable justification cannot be found.

Experience has humbled me enough to let me realize the specific limitations of reason. Just as matter misplaced becomes dirt, reason misused becomes lunacy. If we but render unto Caesar that which is Caesar's, all would be well.

5. The Limitations of Intellect

There is something infinitely higher than intellect that rules us, as even the skeptics. Their skepticism and philosophy do not help them in the critical period of their lives. They need something better, something outside them. And so if some one puts a conundrum before me, I say to him, "You are not going to know the meaning of God or prayer unless you reduce yourself to a cipher. You must be humble enough to see that in spite of your greatness and gigantic intellect you are but a speck in the universe. A merely intellectual conception of things of life is not enough. It is the spiritual conception which eludes the intellect, and which alone can give one satisfaction."

Even moneyed men have critical periods in their lives. Though they are surrounded by everything that money can buy and affection can give, they find at certain moments their lives utterly distracted. It is in these moments that we have a glimpse of God, a vision of him who is guiding every one of our steps.

Intellect takes us along, in the battle of life, to a certain extent, but at the crucial moment fails us. Faith transcends reason. It is when the horizon is the darkest and our human reason is beaten down to the ground, that faith shines the brightest and comes to our rescue. It is such faith that our youth requires and this comes when one has shed all pride of intellect and surrendered oneself entirely to his will.

6. Have Childlike Faith

I would have brushed aside all rational explanations, and begin with a simple childlike faith in God. If I exist God exists. With me it is a necessity of my being as it is with millions. They may not be able to talk about it, but from their lives you can see that it is a part of their life. I am only asking you to restore the belief that has been undermined. In order to do so you have to unlearn a lot of literature that dazzles your intelligence and throws you off your feet. Start with the faith which is also a token of humility and an admission that we know nothing, that we are less than atoms in this universe. We are less than atoms, I say, because the atom obeys the law of its being, whereas, we, in the insolence of our ignorance, deny the law of nature. But I have no argument to address to those who have no faith.

I claim to be a man of faith and prayer, and even if I were to be cut to pieces, I trust God would give me the strength not to deny him, but to assert that he is.... I am surer of his existence than of the fact that you and I are sitting in this room. Then I can also testify that I may live without air and water but not without him. You may pluck out my eyes, but that cannot kill me. You may chop off my nose, but that will not kill me. But blast my faith in God, and I am dead. You may call this a superstition, but I confess it is a superstition that I hug, even as I used to hug the name of Rama in my childhood when there was any cause of danger or alarm.

7. *The Power of Living Faith*

We want the steady light, the infallible light of religious faith; not faith which merely appeals to the intelligence, but a faith which is indelibly inscribed on the heart. First we want to realize our religious consciousness, and immediately we have done that, the whole department of life is open to us; and it should then be a sacred privilege of all, so that when young men grow to manhood they may do so properly equipped to battle with life.

It is faith that steers us through stormy seas; faith that moves mountains, and faith that jumps across the ocean. That faith is nothing but a living and wide-awake consciousness of God within. He who has achieved that faith wants nothing. Bodily diseased, he is spiritually healthy; physically poor, he rolls in spiritual riches.

8. How to Acquire Faith

Faith cannot be acquired by force of intellect. It comes but slowly, after deep meditation and continuous practice. We pray, sing hymns, read books, seek the association of men of God, and perform the spinning sacrifice in order to attain that faith.

Prayer

1. The Nature of Prayer

The divine mind is unchangeable, but that divinity is in everyone and everything, animate and inanimate. The meaning of prayer is that I want to invoke that divinity in me.... I beg it of myself, of my higher self, the real self, with which I have not yet achieved complete identification. You may, therefore, describe it as a continual longing to lose myself in the divinity which comprises all.

I pray to God who exists somewhere in the clouds, and the more distant he is, the greater is my longing for him, and I find myself in his presence in thought. And thought, you know, has a greater velocity than light. Therefore, the distance between me and him though so incalculably great, is obliterated.

2. The Source of Peace and Light

There is an eternal struggle raging in man's breast between the powers of darkness and light, and he who has the sheet-anchor of prayer to rely upon, will not be a victim to powers of darkness. The man of prayer will be at peace with himself and with the whole world, and the man who goes about the affairs of world without a prayerful heart will be miserable and will also make the world miserable.

It is a universal experience that every calamity brings a sensible man down on his knees. He thinks that it is God's answer to his sins and he must henceforth behave better. His sins have left him hopelessly weak and in his weakness he cries out God for help. Thus millions of human beings used their personal calamities for self-improvement.

Prayer is the only means of bringing about orderliness and peace and repose in our daily acts.

3. The Essence and Power of Prayer

He who hungers for the awakening of the divine in him must fall back on prayer.... But it is not a repetition of an empty formula. It is better in prayer to have a heart without words than words without heart. It must be in clear response to the spirit which hungers for it. And even as a hungry man relishes a hearty meal, a hungry soul will relish a heartfelt prayer. And I am giving you a bit of my experience and that of my companions when I say that he who has experienced the magic of prayer, may do without food for days together, but not a single moment without prayer. For without prayer there is no peace.

Prayer is no flight of eloquence. It is no lip-homage. It springs from the heart. If, therefore, we achieve that purity of the heart, when it is emptied of all but love, if we keep all the chords in proper tune, they "trembling pass in music out of sight." Prayer needs no speech. I have not the slightest doubt that prayer is an unfailing means of cleansing the heart of passions. But it must be combined with utmost humility.

Our prayer is a heart-search. It is a reminder to ourselves that we are helpless without his support. No effort is complete without prayer, without a definite recognition that the best human endeavor is of no effect if it has not God's blessings behind it. Prayer is a call to humility. It is a call to self-purification.

4. Patience Is Necessary for Success

Real prayer is an absolute shield and protection against ... evils. Success does not always attend the very first effort at such a living prayer. We have to strive against ourselves, we have to believe in spite of ourselves, because months are as our years. We have, therefore, to cultivate illimitable patience if we will realize the efficacy of prayer. There will be darkness, disappointment and even worse; but we must have courage enough to battle against all these and not succumb to cowardice. There is no such thing as retreat for a man of prayer.

It may take time for the recitation to come from the heart, even as a seed sown has to be nurtured and bears fruit only in due season. If the desire to have God within us is there, progress, however slow, is bound to be. Man cannot be transformed from bad to good overnight. God does not exercise magic. He too is within his own law. His law, however, is different from the law of the state. There may be mistakes in the latter but God cannot err. If he were to go beyond the limits of his law, the world would be lost. He is changeless, unchanging, unequaled, the same yesterday, today, and forever. His law is written on the tablets of their hearts. They could become changed men and women only if they had the desire of reform and if they were prepared for ceaseless endeavor.

5. The Period of Prayer

There can be no fixed rule laid down as to the time these devotional acts should take place. It depends upon individual temperaments. There are precious moments in one's daily life. The exercises are intended to sober and humble us and enable us to realize that nothing happens without his will and that we are but "clay in the hands of the Potter." These are moments when one reviews one's immediate past, confesses one's weaknesses, asks for forgiveness and strength to be and to do better. One minute may be enough for some; twenty-four hours would be too little for others.

For those who are filled with the presence of God in them, to labor is to pray. The life is one continuous prayer or act of worship. For those who act only to sin, to indulge themselves and to live for self, no time is too much. If they had patience and faith and the will to be pure, they would pray till they feel the definite purifying presence of God within them. For us ordinary mortals there must be a middle path between these two extremes. We are not so exalted as to be able to say that all our acts are a dedication, nor, perhaps, are we so far gone as to living purely for self. Hence have all religions set apart times for general devotion.

6. Begin and Close the Day with Prayer

I believe that prayer is the very soul and essence of religion, and therefore prayer must be the very core of the life of man. . . .

Begin, therefore, your day with prayer, and make it so soulful that it may remain with you until evening. Close the day with prayer so that you may have a peaceful night free from dreams and nightmares. Do not worry about the forms. Let it be any form; it should be such as can put us in communion with the divine. Only let not the spirit wander while the words of prayer run on out of your mouth.

Meditation and the Mantram

1. The Virtue of Silence

Experience has taught me that silence is part of the spiritual discipline of a votary of truth.... When one comes to think of it, one cannot help feeling that nearly half the misery of the world would disappear if we, fretting mortals, knew the virtue of silence. Before modern civilization came upon us, at least six to eight hours of silence out of twenty-four were vouchsafed to us. Modern civilization has taught us to convert night into day and golden silence into brazen din and noise. What a great thing it would be if we in our busy lives, could retire into ourselves each day, for at least a couple of hours, and prepare our minds to listen to the voice of the great silence. The divine radio is always singing if we could only make ourselves ready to listen to it, but it is impossible to listen without silence. St. Teresa has used a charming image to sum up the sweet result of silence:

> You will at once feel your senses gather themselves together; they seem like bees which return to the hive and they shut themselves up from work, without effort or care on your

part. God thus rewards the violence which your soul has been doing to itself, and gives to it such a domination over the senses that a sign is enough, when it desires to recollect itself, for them to obey and go gather themselves together. At the first call of the will, they come back more and more quickly. At last after many and many exercises of this kind, God disposes them to a state of absolute repose and of perfect contemplation.

2. Silence Facilitates Communion with God

Silence has now become both a physical and spiritual necessity for me. Originally it was taken to relieve the sense of pressure. Then I wanted time for writing. After, however, I had practiced it for sometime, I saw the spiritual value of it. It suddenly flashed across my mind that that was the time when I could best hold communion with God. And now I feel as though I was naturally built for silence.

Silence is a great help to a seeker after truth like myself. In the attitude of silence the soul finds the path in a clearer light, and what is elusive and deceptive resolves itself into crystal clearness. Our life is long and arduous quest after truth and the soul requires inward restfulness to attain its full height.

3. True Meditation

True meditation consists in closing the eyes and ears of the mind to all else except the object of one's devotion. Hence, the closing of the eyes during prayers is an aid to such concentration. Man's conception of God is naturally limited. Each one has, therefore, to think of him as best appears to him, provided that the conception is pure and uplifting.

4. The Power of God's Name

Rama is the strength of the weak. This strength is not to be obtained by taking up arms or by similar means. It is to be had by throwing oneself on his name. Rama is but a synonym of God. You may say God or Allah or whatever other name you like, but the moment you trust naught but him, you are strong. All disappointment disappears.

Ramanama [the repetition of God's name] is an alchemy such as can transform the body. The conservation of vital energy has been likened to accumulated wealth, but it is in the power of Ramanama alone to make it a running stream of ever-increasing spiritual strength, ultimately making a fall impossible. Just as the body cannot exist without blood, so the soul needs the matchless and pure strength of faith. This strength can renovate the weakness of all man's physical organs.

That is why it is said that when Ramanama is enshrined in the heart, it means the rebirth of man. This law applies to the young, old, man, and woman alike.

5. Take the Name with Every Breath

Though my reason and heart long ago realized the highest attribute and name of God as truth, I recognize truth by the name of Rama. In the darkest hour of my trial, that one name has saved me and is still saving me.

When a child, my nurse taught me to repeat Ramanama whenever I felt afraid or miserable, and it has been second nature with me, with growing knowledge and advancing years. I may even say that the word is in my heart, if not actually on my lips, all the twenty-four hours. It has been my savior and I am ever stayed on it.

What is the mark of a man who has Rama enshrined in his heart? Such a man will take God's name with every breath. His Rama will be awake even whilst the body is asleep. Rama will be always with him in whatever he does. The real death for such a devoted man will be loss of this sacred companionship.

A devotee of Rama may be said to be the same as the steadfast one—*Sthitaprajna*—of the Bhagavad Gita. He will live in the consciousness of the soul and look to the care, first and last, of the indweller. Such a man will take God's name with every breath.

6. Blessings of Ramanama

My Rama ... is not the historical Rama. He is the eternal, the unborn, the one without a second. Him alone I worship.

A Christian may find the same solace from the repetition of the name of Jesus and a Muslim from the name of Allah. All these things have the same implications, and they produce identical results. Only the repetition must not be a lip-expression, but part of your very being.

I have said that to take Ramanama from the heart means deriving help from an incomparable power. The atom bomb is as nothing compared with it. This power is capable of removing all pain.

There is no doubt whatsoever that Ramanama contains all the power that is attributed to it. No one can by mere wishing enshrine Ramanama in his heart. Untiring effort is required, as also patience. What an amount of labor and patience have been lavished by men to acquire the nonexistent philosopher's stone? Surely, God's name is of infinitely richer value.

With my hand on my breast, I can say that not a minute in my life am I forgetful of God.

Self-Surrender

1. Surrender Brings Joy

Who am I? I have no strength save what God gives me. I have no authority over my countrymen save the purely moral. If he holds me to be a pure instrument for the spread of nonviolence, he will give me the strength and show me the way. My greatest weapon is mute prayer. The cause of peace is, therefore, in God's good hands. Nothing can happen but by his will expressed in his eternal, changeless law, which is he. We neither know him nor his law, save through the glass darkly. But the faint glimpse of the law is sufficient to fill me with joy, hope, and faith in the future.

I must go with God as my only guide. He is a jealous Lord. He will allow no one to share his authority. One has, therefore to appear before him in all one's meekness, empty-handed, and in a spirit of full surrender, and he enables you to stand before the whole world and protects you from all harm.

I have been a willing slave to this most exacting master for more than half a century. His voice has been increasingly audible as years have rolled by. He has never forsaken me in my darkest hour. He has saved me often against myself and left me not a vestige of independence. The greater the surrender to him the greater has been my joy.

2. God Moves and Protects All

We are but straws in the hands of God. He alone can blow us where he pleases. We cannot oppose his wish.

If we can but throw ourselves into his lap as our only help, we shall come out scatheless through every ordeal. If nothing happens without his permission, where is the difficulty in believing that he is trying us? I would take our complaints to him for so cruelly trying us. And he will soothe us and forgive us if we will but trust him.

We must learn, each one of us, to stand alone. God only is our infallible and eternal guide.... God helps the helpless, not those who believe they can do something. Those who put their implicit faith in him cannot but reach their aims.

No one can see God face to face who has aught of an "I" in him. He must become a cipher if he would see God. Who shall dare say in this storm-tossed universe, "I have won"? God triumphs in us, never we.

3. Dedicate All to God

In a moment of introspection, the poet asks himself:

> O man, why have you left off taking God's name?
> You have not given up anger or lust or greed,
> But you have forgotten truth.
> What a tragedy to save worthless pennies,
> And to let go the priceless gem of God's love.
> O Fool, renounce all vanities,
> And throw yourself on the grace of God alone.

This does not mean that if one has wealth, it should be thrown away, and wife and children should be turned out of doors. It simply means that one must give up attachment to these things and dedicate one's all to God and make use of his gifts to serve him only. It also means that if we take his name with all our being, we are automatically weaned from all lust, untruth, and baser passions.

We must eternally sing his praise and do his will. Let us dance to the tune of his *bansi* [flute] and all would be well.

Part Four
Spiritual Experience

Some Aspects of Experience

1. The Blessed Feeling of God's Presence

I believe it to be possible for every human being to attain that blessed and indescribable state in which he feels within himself the presence of God to the exclusion of everything else.

I hold that complete realization is impossible in this embodied life. Nor is it necessary. A living immovable faith is all that is required for reaching the full spiritual height attainable by human beings. God is not outside the earthly case of ours. Therefore exterior proof is not of much avail, if at all. We must ever fail to perceive him through the senses, because he is beyond them. We can feel him if we will but withdraw ourselves from the senses.

Seeing God face to face is to feel that he is enthroned in our hearts, even as a child feels a mother's affection without needing any demonstration. Does a child reason out the existence of a mother's love? Can he prove it to others? He triumphantly declares, "It is." So must it be with the existence of God. He defies reason. But he is experienced. Let us not reject the experience of

Tulsidas, Chaitanya, Ramdas, and a host of other spiritual teachers, even as we do not reject that of mundane teachers.

There is not a moment when I do not feel the presence of a witness, whose eye misses nothing and with whom I strive to keep in tune.

If I did not feel the presence of God within me, 1 see so much of misery and disappointment everyday that I would be a raving maniac and my destination would be the [River] Hoogli.

2. The Vision of God

What is the vision of God? It does not mean seeing something with the physical eye or witnessing a miracle. Seeing God means realization of the fact that God abides in our hearts. The yearning must persist until one has attained this realization, and will vanish upon realization. Realization is the final fruit of constant effort. God is there in the tabernacle of the heart.

We cannot see God with these eyes. God is spirit without body and is, therefore, visible only to the eye of faith. If there are no evil thoughts troubling our mind, and no fears, but constant cheerfulness in our heart, that is an indication of God's presence in ourselves. Indeed he is there at all times, but we fail to notice his presence as we have no faith, and thus undergo much suffering. When once we have cultivated real faith, calamities cease to upset us.

One who looks upon the universe as various facets of God will certainly have the beatific vision. All our knowledge and spiritual exercises are fruitless, so long as we have not had this vision.

When I admire the wonder of a sunset or the beauty of the moon, my soul expands in worship of the creator. I try to see him and his mercies in all these creations.

3. His Light and Music

The fleeting glimpses that I have been able to have of truth can hardly convey an idea of the indescribable luster of truth, a million times more intense than that of the Sun we daily see with our eyes. In fact, what I have caught is only the faintest glimmer of that mighty effulgence. I feel the warmth and sunshine of his presence.

The Sun in Heaven fills the whole universe with its life-giving warmth. But if one went too near it, it would consume him to ashes. Even so, it is with godhead. We become godlike to the extent we realize nonviolence; but we never become wholly God.

My firm belief is that he reveals himself daily to every

human being, but we shut our ears to the "still small voice." We shut our eyes to the pillar of fire in front of us. I realize his omnipresence.

The divine music is incessantly going on within ourselves; but the loud senses drown the delicate music, which is unlike, and infinitely superior to, any we can perceive or hear with our senses.

When this inner light corresponds with the promptings of the smaller inner voice, then that flash has a mark of inspiration.

4. The Inner Voice

The inner voice defies description. But sometimes we do feel that we receive an inspiration from within. The time when I learnt to recognize it may be called my prayer time, say about 1906. I recollect it. For the rest, never did I feel at any time in my life that I had some new experience. My spiritual growth has been unnoticed, like the growth of hair on our heads.

Nobody has, to my knowledge, questioned the possibility of the inner voice speaking to some, and it is a gain to the world even if one person's claim to speak under the authority of the inner voice can be really sustained.

Many may make the claim, but not all will be able

to substantiate it. But it cannot and ought not to be suppressed for the sake of preventing false claimants. There is no danger whatsoever if many people could truthfully represent the inner voice. But unfortunately there is no remedy against hypocrisy. Virtue must not be suppressed because many will feign it. Men have always been found throughout the world claiming to speak for the inner voice. But no harm has yet overtaken the world through their short-lived activities.

Before one is able to listen to that voice, one has to go through a long and severe course of training, and when it is the inner voice that speaks, it is unmistakable. The world cannot successfully be fooled for all time. There is, therefore, no danger of anarchy setting in because an humble man like me will not be suppressed, and will dare to claim the authority of the inner voice when he believes that he has heard it.

Man is a fallible being. He can never be sure of his steps. What he may regard as an answer to prayer may be an echo of his pride. For infallible guidance man has to have a perfectly innocent heart incapable of evil. I can lay no such claim. Mine is a struggling, striving, erring, imperfect soul.

5. Divine Messages

On the night of April 28, 1933, Gandhi was awakened in his
quarters at Yeravda Central Prison by the voice of God. He was
urged to undertake a twenty-one day fast for self-purification, in order
to advance the cause of the underclass of Hindu society, the "untouch-
ables." On May 8, Gandhi was released from prison as his fast
began; it ended May 29.

One experience stands quite distinctly in my memory.
It relates to my twenty-one days' fast for the removal
of untouchability. I had gone to sleep the night before
without the slightest idea of having to declare a fast
the next morning. At about twelve o'clock in the night
something wakes me up suddenly and some voice—
within or without, I cannot say—whispers, "Thou
must go on fast." "How many days?" I ask. It says,
"Twenty-one days." "When does it begin?" I ask. It
says, "You begin tomorrow." I went quietly off to sleep
after making the decision. I did not tell anything to
my companions until after the morning prayer. I placed
into their hands a slip of paper announcing my decision
and asking them not to argue with me as the decision
was irrevocable. Well, the doctors thought that I would
not survive the fast. But something within me said I
would and that I must go forward. That kind of experience has never in my life happened before or after
that date.

The first question that has puzzled many is about the voice of God. What was it? What did I hear?' Was there any person I saw? If not, how was the voice conveyed to me? These are pertinent questions.

I saw no form. I have never tried for it, for I have always believed God to be without form. But what I did hear was like a voice from afar and yet quite near. It was as unmistakable as some human voice, definitely speaking to me, and irresistible. I was not dreaming at the time I heard the voice. The hearing of the voice was preceded by a terrific struggle within me. Suddenly the voice came upon me. I listened, made certain that it was the voice and the struggle ceased. I was calm. The determination was made accordingly, the date and the hour of the fast fixed. Joy came over me. This was between eleven and twelve midnight. I felt refreshed.

Could I give any further evidence that it was truly the voice I heard and that it was not an echo of my own heated imagination? I have no further evidence to convince the skeptic. He is free to say it was all self-delusion or hallucination. It may well have been so. I can offer no proof to the contrary. But I can say this: that not the unanimous verdict of the whole world against me could shake me from the belief that what I heard was the true voice of God.... For me the voice was more real than my existence.

This I know: that all that glitters is not gold, and also that if a man has really heard the voice of God, there is no sliding back, just as there is no forgetting it by one who had learnt to swim. The listening in must make people's lives daily richer and richer.

6. *An Ideal Sage*

That man alone can be called truly religious or moral whose mind is not tainted with hatred or selfishness, and who leads a life of absolute purity and of disinterested service; and that man alone can be called truly wealthy or happy either. Only such a man can do good to mankind; for truth is the foundation of all that is good and great. To a true servant of humanity, the question never arises as to the best form of service. When we have realized the majesty of the moral law, we shall see how little our happiness or unhappiness depends on health and success and fame and the like. As has been said by Emerson, "Even the pains and griefs of good men contribute to their happiness, while even the wealth and fame of bad men cause misery to themselves as well as to the world." "Seek ye first the kingdom of God, and his righteousness and all other things shall be added unto you."

He is a real devotee who is jealous of none, who is a fount of mercy, who is without egoism, who treats alike cold and heat, happiness and misery, who is ever forgiving, who is always contented, whose resolutions are firm, who has dedicated mind and soul to God, who causes no dread, who is not afraid of others, who is free from exultation, sorrow, and fear, who is pure, who is versed in action and yet remains unaffected by it, who renounces all fruit, good or bad, who treats friend and foe alike, who is untouched by respect or disrespect, who is not puffed up with praise, who does not go under when people speak ill of him, who loves silence and solitude, who has disciplined reason.

The yogi is, therefore, one who reflects all these attributes in his life; who, in the midst of raging storm and blinding spray, will keep his vision of the Sun undisturbed; who will look difficulties and death in the face; who goes with the same mind to the shambles and the scaffold; and whose mind is so serene that thunder rocks him to sleep.

Sources

A—*Autobiography*
CGGVL—Conversations of Gandhiji, quoted in *Gandhiji's View of Life*
EF—*Epic Fast*
ER—*Ethical Religion*
FPJ—*Free Press Journal*
FYM—*From Yeravda Mandir*
G—*Gandhiji*, published in 1944, on Gandhiji's 75th Birthday.
GC—*Gandhiji in Ceylon*
GH—*Guide to Health*
GS—*Gospel of Selfless Action* or *The Gita According to Gandhi*, by M. Desai
H—*Harijan*
MD—*The Diary of Mahadev Desai, Vol. I*
SW—*Speeches and Writings of Mahatma Gandhi*
Y—*Young India*

God

1. Y 9-25-24; H 3-13-37
2. H 7-14-46
3. Y 10-11-28; H 11-24-46;
   H 6-22-47; H 3-28-53; Y
   10-11-28
4. Y 10-11-28; H 8-24-47
5. A p. 6; Y 3-5-25
6. Y 7-30-39
7. H 3-23-40; Y 3-9-22
8. Y 3-9-22; Y 1-21-26;
   SW p. 1069
9. H 3-3-46; Y 9-24-25;
   H 8-18-46; Y 5-5-27
10. H 6-22-47

Soul

1. H 6-3-39
2. H 7-8-36
3. FYM p. 30
4. Y 3-12-20; G p. 389;
   Y 10-20-26
5. Y 6-3-26; H 3-23-40;
   H 11-21-36
6. ER p. 3; H 4-4-36;
   Y 9-20-28; Y 3-9-22

World

1. H 5-26-46
2. Y 3-2-22; Y 5-13-26
3. H 9-7-35; Y 10-11-28

4. CCGVL p. 49
5. H 2-20-37; C.G.G.V.L
   p. 47; CGGVL p. 49
6. H 6-15-35

Truth

1. Y 12-31-31; Y 7-30-31
2. GH p. 114
3. Y 7-30-31; H 12-10-38;
   A p. 84
4. H 6-2-46
5. Y 7-30-31; FYM p. 3

Love

1. MD p. 54; Y 9-20-28
2. Y 5-5-20
3. H 9-26-36; Y 10-23-24;
   Y 5-10-19
4. Y 5-10-19; H 9-15-40
5. Y 6-24-26; Y 8-11-20;
   H 8-11-40; H 5-7-47

Self-Restraint

1. Y 1-23-30
2. GH p. 131; A p. 392
3. H 11-21-36, FYM p. 19
4. H 7-23-38
5. FYM p. 8; H 4-24-37

Selfless Service

1. H 2-24-46; FYM p. 17
2. H 8-29-36
3. H 8-22-39
4. Y 4-3-24

Faith

1. H 4-25-36; H 6-22-47
2. H 9-12-34
3. H 6-21-27
4. H 3-6-37; Y 6-24-26;
   Y 10-14-26
5. H 8-19-39; Y 6-21-29
6. Y 9-24-31; Y 12-8-27;
   H 5-14-38
7. SW Speech on 2-16-16 at
   YMCA; Y 9-24-25
8. G p. 397

Prayer

1. H 3-19-39
2. Y 1-30-30; H 8-18-46;
   Y 1-30-30
3. Y 1-23-33; A p. 96; H
   6-8-35
4. Y 12-20-28; H 5-19-46
5. Y 6-10-26
6. Y 1-23-30

Meditation

1. A p.84; H 9-24-38
2. H 1-10-38
3. H 8-18-46
4. Y 6-1-25; H 6-29-47
5. H 8-17-34; H 3-18-33;
   H 6-29-47
6. H 4-28-46; H 12-5-36;
   H 10-13-46; H 2-17-46;
   Y 6-27-27

Dedication

1. H 12-9-39; Y 9-3-31;
   H 5-6-33
2. Y 5-15-24; Y 12-15-21;
   Y 9-29-21; Y 2-23-22;
   Y 11-1-25; Y 6-25-25
3. H 4-28-46; Y 3-5-25

Experience

1. Y 11-17-21; H 6-13-36;
   Y 7-9-25; H 12-24-38;
   Y 8-6-25

2. MD p. 54; MD p. 114;
   MD p.244; Y 11-13-24
3. A p. 615; H 11-12-38;
   Y 5-25-21; H 6-13-36;
   FPJ 1-10-33
4. MD p.275; H 3-18-33;
   Y 9-25-24
5. H 7-8-33; H 12-10-38;
   H 10-7-39
6. ER p. 31; GS p. 126 &
   p. 51

Contributors

Arun Gandhi is the fifth grandson of Mahatma Gandhi. Raised in South Africa at the Phoenix Ashram, a religious community established by his grandfather in 1904, he moved to India as a teenager in 1945, and lived with the Mahatma during the last years of his life. Dr. Gandhi is a former journalist, and with his wife, Sunanda, started India's Center for Social Unity, an organization dedicated to alleviating poverty and caste discrimination. The author of eight books, Dr. Gandhi has been a resident of the United States since 1987. He and his wife are founders of the M. K. Gandhi Institute for Nonviolence at Christian Brothers University in Memphis, Tennessee.

Michael Nagler is Professor Emeritus of Classics and Comparative Literature at the University of California, Berkeley. He is the founder of the University's Peace and Conflict Studies Program, and currently teaches courses in nonviolence and meditation. Dr. Nagler is the author of *America Without Violence*, and, with Eknath Easwaran, an English edition of *The Upanishads*, as well as numerous articles on classics, myth, peace, and mysticism.